Other Books By Jim R. Rogers

Looking Around,
A Selection of Poems

The Incredible Importance of Effective Parenting:
Plain Talk About Raising Children
From a Concerned Field Worker

Geriatric Monologues,
a play adapted from Starts and Stops
still learning, inc., 2016

Starts And Stops Along The Way
*Sharing Some Stuff
From The Road Most Travel*

by
Jim R. Rogers

Pp
PROSEPRESS
www.prosepress.biz

Starts And Stops Along The Way
Copyright © 2012, 2ND Edition, 2016
Jim R. Rogers

All rights reserved.
This publication may not be reproduced, stored in a retrieval system, or transmitted in any form: recording, mechanical, electronic, or photocopy, without written permission of the publisher.
The only exception is brief quotations used in book reviews.

Comments: Contact Jim Rogers at jimrogers@sc.rr.com

ISBN:
Hard cover   978-0-9851889-9-3
Paper Back   978-0-9895042-5-6

Cover Design: Jim R. Rogers,
    Photo by Sally Z. Hare
    Sea View Inn porch, Pawleys Island, SC

Prose Press
Pawleys Island,
South Carolina 29585
prosencons@live.com

Dedicated to

all of you taking the road most travel

and to

daughter Julie Kay
and her son Daniel
my son Kyle

and to

former wives
Shirley and Kelly
brother Bob
sister Gloria

and especially to

my wife
and inspiration,
my teacher, my friend,
the one who holds my heart
and gives me hope

Sally

special thanks to
readers and audiences who have by
your generosity and acceptance
made this 2nd edition possible.

Starts And Stops Along The Way

1.
So This Is It

2.
Seems Like Yesterday

3.
Sit Down And Stay A While

4.
Whose Life Was It Anyway

5.
Ok. Now What

6.
My Time Has Passed

7.
The Road Most Travel

Contents

1.
So This Is It 1

Interview 2
If You're Not Old 2
And Here We Are 3-4
Leave Me Be! 4
Not Yourself 5
Calendar Pages 5
Who Wants To Be Old 6
Starting To Go 6
Not Much Thought 6
Zip Swoosh Zing 7
Pick And Choose 7
AARP Is Our Badge 8
Old Man 9
Magic 9
Both 10
How About Reunions 11
Stuff 12
Which Way 12
Talking Along 13
Feeling The Energy 13
Old Glory 14

Your Turn To Write

2.
Seems Like Yesterday 16

From Birth 17
Out Of The House 18
It Was Supposed To Be 19
Whatever I Have 19
Family 19
When Do You Know 20-21
Decades 21
This I Know For Sure 22
Remember 22
Passion 33
Oldies But Goodies 23
Used To Be 24
Afternoon And Evening Nods 24
Little Things 25
Sides 26
Starts And Stops 372

3.
Sit Down And Stay A While 29

Visits 30
This Is Not Good 30
Love Has Not Been A Stranger 31-32
Will You Remind Me 32
Spooning 33
Bubble Stuff 33
When You Can Stare 34
Finding Joy 34
Temptations 34

Closer 35
Difficult Getting Through 35
PDA 35
Grandchildren 36
Son Told Us Today 36
You'll Tell Me 37
We Did Some Things 38

**4.
Whose Life Was It Anyway!** 39

You 40
He Often Envied 40-41
Think About It 41
Irritations On The Small Stuff 42
OC 42
Hanger Hell 43
Two Seniors 43
Feel Like Screaming 44
Even The Most Intimate 44
And Then 45
This Is The Age 45
Sagging 45
Getting Shorter 46
Pretty Soon 46
When You Get Old 46
TV Is My Challenge 47
It Takes Longer 47
Expand A-Waist 48
Senior Ballet 48
Reinventing Ourselves 48
They Laugh At Us 49

The Older I Get 50
Bothers Me 50
Educate Me? 51
Hair 51
Skin Gets Thin 51
All The $ Went 52
Starts With Squinting 52
For A While 53
Reading 54
Tired Of Doing It 54
Clothes 55
Can't Talk About It 55
Regimen 56-57
Mom Chose Family Dollar Sweats 58
Growing Apart 59
What We Have Become 59
There Is No Bottom 60

A Reminder To Write

**5.
Ok. Now What** 61

Beliefs 62
Home Work 62
Time 63
Brick By Brick 63
Self Help 64
Anthropology Navigator 65
The Cloudy Day Parts 65-68
Good Morning! 69
When I Started Getting Busy 69

Staying So Long 70
Sitting In A Room 71
Who 71
Not Too Concerned 72
Experience Counts For Something 72
Retiree Envy At A Fall Festival 73
Flags Of Our Fathers 74
I'm Not As Good 74
My Hectic Busy Life 75
No News 75
Epiphany On The Roof 76
It's Building 77
Financial 77
Timing 78
Old People Are Problems 78
Dogs 79
Inside Work 80
Can't Don't 80
I Know I'm Right 80
All My Life 81
Just Some Ramblings 82-93

6.
My Time Has Passed 94

Volunteer 95
Something So Mundane 95
I Cry Over What Should Be 96
I'm Not Dead 96
Still Doing 96
Who Served 97
We Matter 97

So 98
They're Gone Under 99
There's A Picture Of Me 99
When We Start Reflecting 100-101
We Are Here To Grow 101
Waiting 102
When You Have Nothing To Do 102
Criticize 103
So Much To Do 103
Gone 103
Paralyzed 104
Took The Less Traveled Path 104
Will 104
Three Things 105
Here's One 105
Anger 105
What I Owe 106
Luck 107

7.
The Road Most Travel 108

The Only Way 109
Best Friends 110
New Best Friends 110
One 111
We Don't Know It 111
When Her Mother Was Sick 112
Thinking 113
Old Folks Are Slow To Panic 114
Children 114
Ailments Abound 115

Friends No More 115
Getting Harder To Remember 116
Visiting Questions Unanswered 115
All The Time We Hear It 117
She Faded 117
Giving Up Giving In 117
What You Put In 118
Place 118
How We Do It 119
She Settled In To Die 119
Home 120
Everybody 121
Dependent 121
Love Life 121
Last Night 122
I'm Not Ready 123
Don't Care For Me 124
Fear Is A Scary Thing 124
How To Keep Going 125
About That Doctor Thing 125
Clichés 126
Let's Say 127
Closets 128
That's It 129

1.

So This Is It

Interview
Who do you want to read this?
Everybody
What do you want them to get out of it?
Anything they can find
But it's not complex… it's not mysterious
It's not academic or scientific or award winning
not even a single contest prize.
Should be simple
So more will understand
Don't want them to have to search for it
Figure it out
I want them to find it easily
Feel good about the finding
and then do something.
That's it?
That's it.

If You're Not Old, Stop
Don't read this
You won't understand it.
Save it till you can
Or give it to someone who
Might
Be Old
Then they can give it back to you
When you're old
With input.
Old? Only you know.
For me
Invisible
Even in crowded rooms
Profound! words of wisdom ignored
Less profound
Not even heard
Eyes and ears turned away
Too old to contribute

Or to talk about
Current issues
They think we think how we used to do it
Is the only way
New ideas
I've had none
No
I stopped learning and
Did it the way I always did
Oh yeah. Sure.
Some do
Some don't
Respectful
Almost
Condescending, placating but then
Accepting it seems
Welcome is phony
Here's something you can do for us
We need a senior on our board.

And Here We Are
On the way
To being old
Released from
Corporate structure
Mandates
Orders
Expectations
Raising children
Raising cane
And all that required stuff of the early years.
What will it mean?
We don't know
We've never been here before
Others have but
That's them

Now it's us
Set free to be
Younger, healthier
Empty nestier
For now.
Decisions still
But new, like they say
Rearranging
The deck chairs on the Titanic
Where to go, Downsize. Upsize
Gated Apartment, Condo
Parent house out back or attached
Retirement community
The village
The dreaded facility with nurses.
Real old folk
Yearn to stay
Home values down
Once a second floor, status
Now, A Challenge
Smart
Senior Friendly Home
Comfort is what we want
Something more
Than shelter
Where we can be us
Where we have
Memories.
Where we can
Age in place
Where we can be
Old Folks AT Home

Leave Me Be!
But
don't leave me
alone

       Not Yourself
       You're not acting like
       yourself
       they said.
     I've never been who I am before,
    so I don't know if I am myself
   or not.
The problem is that
you don't know what you want to be when you
grow up until you grow up and then
it's most likely too late to start.
Unless it's not.

Calendar Pages.
One by one
They come
And go.
They don't mean
Anything at all
Unless we
Want them to
In the mind
In the heart
In the desire
In the joy of
Being alive
To turn
Another page.

Who Wants To Be Old
        Not he
        Not she
        Not I
        Not we
        But we are.
        So we
        be.

    Starting To Go
You feel it
You know.
Oh no!
Some go soon
Others wait
Why is that?
Learning how to live with
Loss.
Learning what we
Have to. I guess.

Not Much Thought
at the time
about who our children would be.
Not much effort to help them get there.
Here.
Maybe too late to do much now.
Maybe not.

Zip! Swoosh! Zing!
Those are the sounds it made as it went by.
It started slow enough, young eyes
sparkling with discovery
finding the joy in it wanting each day to last
longer than the one before
especially summer.
Oh, they did drag sometimes, mostly when you wanted
to date, to drive, to smoke, to drink,
to be left alone.
And then you are. How fast it goes now.
Twice the speed of light.
Hard not to fall off.
Not what you thought.
Not what you dreamed.
Not where you wanted to be
But here you are.
So.
Cares get more refined.
Time is told in different ticks and tocks.
No stones left to un-turn.
Shirts and pants don't match and once I wore
two different shoes
No one noticed.

Pick And Choose
That's what aging offers.
Can't do it all any more
don't even try
only so many hours,
so many weeks
so many days and nights to go
so many choices get slimmed down
to the few that we want to do
be with the ones we want to be with

hug only those who know we mean it
cut the do list down to done
many times not, but never again
routines go out, take risks for once
be late sometime but be sorry, too
since we still respect and get it back.
Idle hours just staring into space
they think
really just staring into past
looking to tomorrows, to what's still there.
So spend the time that's left
the way we want to spend it
don't be rude or sharp of tongue
stay polite and caring, but
be bold and not ashamed to let
the ones that count
count. Just make sure they know it.

AARP Is Our Badge
to inform, to advocate
guide our paths away from ignorance
with dignity, with respect
like 91% of us over 65
have at least one chronic condition!
(Well, thanks for that aarp)
And sell us really tacky mail order clothes
shoes that don't need lacing.
Sex aids! Because it's never too late
And sticks with springs and claws for reaching
where our bodies just won't go.

Old Man
When we watched the playback of the Christmas
video it hit me over the head like a ton of bricks
That was me. The old man.
While I wasn't looking I had aged
I had not been unhappy really
and I had been healthy
and I had been doing my work well and supported
and loved
so how the hell did I get so old so fast.
I knew it was time for me to actually do something
with my life
fulfill my purpose
make a real difference
do something for god's sake
or one morning I would wake up dead
with the excuse that I had been too busy
or I really didn't know what to do
or how to do it so
I did something else.

Magic
Eating in my chair, watching TV
Pillow as my makeshift table
Napkins, towels, bib
Trying hard, aware, careful even, but
Still spill food on my just cleaned shirt
Again.

Both
It's hard not being who I was
but now it's so.
I still am some
at least the parts that count
other things don't and it's a good thing
since hair is gone, muscle is less, get up and go is missing,
joints need oil.
Age is sneaky
you know it's back there lurking, waiting
all of a sudden, overnight
there it is in the mirror wrapped around you
like a bad fitting coat.
It's in others' eyes
it's the disappear potion
and it works
as you are no longer seen.
No one takes you seriously
old stories are just that
and they don't count for much
except to you.
Only a few regrets
and only because of sadness
hurt, pain you may have caused
and you have no idea about
what's next.
How could you really
how could anybody?
No one has been there to tell it
to share it
So you live each hour
like the last and mull
trying not to hurt again
or end up on the line somewhere
believing that what has been
was a cruel joke or
an extraordinary privilege.
Of course. It's Both.

How About Reunions

Went to one
Knew no one
Until
Faces came
Through
Wrinkles
Spots
Sag
Time
And there
They were
Classmates
Again
Shining
Smiling
Faking
Appearing
In spite of
It.

Stuff
from years
Stacks and
Layers
From room to room
And paths
And detours
To bed
To the refrigerator
What to do
Where to go
Who wants
What's there
On the walls
In the halls
Shelves so full
Boxes now
What to do
Out they go
Here I stay.

Which Way
I could have done this or
I could have done that
but not both
how the hell do we choose?
We don't
It chooses us.

Talking Along
And
    Bam!
Can't think
Of the next
Word.
Stalled
In mid sentence
While they wait
To see
If I can
Make it.

Feeling The Energy
draining out
Meds galore
To plug the dike
A tug of war
Science
Vs.
Nature
Who will win
Who do you think.

Old Glory
Smiles, and happy times and much more than a lot not encumbered.

They rested there reclined in the folds of my mind knowing but not knowing that someday they would stretch and unfurl once again to wave in the winds of life.

It feels good to fly, to be exposed to the elements, to sag one minute only to burst forth with currents of emotion not allowed to be for fear of pain, for fear of another loss, a loss of something never had.

Notice the edges ... wear, starting to tear, eating into the very heart of the design across which stitches and patches have been applied holding it together for yet another reveille and taps hoping for a longer day to separate the two and sunshine is best
    it only fades the colors.
Flag bearer, flag bearer feel how soft I am
how thin I am, sometimes.
   You as one so close can almost see clear through.

      Saluted.
      Applauded.
      Honored.
      Protected.
      Pitied.
      Extended.
    Retired.

Hang it on a flat wall In the den or frame it behind glass.
No more wind.
No more sunshine.
Only pool and sometime parties, pro bowls and empty tv.
Occasionally
    an admiring eye who sees
what once was there.

YOUR TURN!

I can almost hear you saying,

"I can do this stuff."

And you are right. You can.

So I have included a few blank

pages at the end of the last section

offering you some space for your

own thoughts, your own memories

in your own words on your

own aging journey.

Have fun. I did.

2.

Seems Like Yesterday

From Birth
there was sunshine
and happy days
and Twain friends

and caring parents
friendly neighbors
inspiring teachers
and grandstand cheers

The world was small
and simple
complications were
way off somewhere.

Special and
destined to be
somebody different
than they had ever known

Everybody thought it
and he took it
and began the race
that he knew nothing about

Ill prepared
but eager
full of hope
he took his steps.

Tomorrows
became todays
became the past
and what of
the life?

Out Of The House
I went
away from all
that I knew
feeling the world
like never before
eyes wide
heart ready
brain growing.
Each one found
fresh
exciting
worrisome
then scary
then too many
one two three
and more
teachers
giving
getting some
but not enough
one so odd and
would not fit
one so bright so right
so wrong
maybe home
was best
no way it's so
just go and go and grow.

It Was Supposed To Be
simple, clear, direct, and even easy.
But it just got complicated.
There was no way a young and idealistic boy
from a Norman Rockwell town could have
prepared for what he got.
On the Job training.
Why do we wait so long
before we start telling the truth?
Maybe it takes that long
to figure it out.

Whatever I have
Is what I've got
No more No less
It's mine
I worked hard
Lived long Loved many Lost some
Laughed a lot
And cried.
Whatever I have
It's mine
Whatever it is.

Family
Glue
That holds
Us together
Gets
Too hot and
Melts
And the
Pieces
Fall
Apart
But
Stay
Sticky.

When Do You Know
 it's time for a change.
When does the idea first appear?

A distant spot of sail on the mind's horizon gliding slowly
toward you getting fuller and bigger and closer and stronger
as it sensitizes your knowing of the wind

Does it grow like a seed in the ground, getting larger and
healthier as its environment of need waters and nurtures it to
blossom and beautifully lulls you into the notion that you had
better move from where you are. Sometime soon.

Or maybe it starts as a mental cold sore, causing just a hint of
the pain that is to come unless you do something
but of course you don't know all that unless you've
gone through such change before and if you have
then why are you letting yourself in for all that shit again?

 It could be that you are just sick and tired of
being sick and tired as the 12 steppers say.
You could be just stuck in a mud rut, adjusted to the goo and
slow movement and not want to do anything
but stay stuck.

Then, there's that classic cliché
when the pain of staying is worse than the pain of leaving
That's when you have to change
To do otherwise would be totally foolish
And yet being foolish doesn't seem to matter
Since when I am deep into dysfunctional comfort
I don't care if I'm foolish or not
I care about whether I'm happy or not.
But even then, happiness is so fleeting
one minute high, another low
I always feel empty when I'm happy…and guilty
It won't last long and there are so many others who aren't.
So, I don't do anything.

They say that's a decision.
It is just too much trouble.
I don't think I can change.
Not if my life depends on it. Maybe it does. Naa.
What's the big deal?
I'm just hot that's all
and I need to cool this room down.
Now let's see. Is it up to cool or down to cool?
Never can get that straight.
Should I take a chance, or
wait for somebody who knows?

I think I'll wait.
For now.
Maybe.

Decades
So many
So many
Of us
So many
Paths
We took
So many
Stories
To tell
So much
Happened
In our
Decades
So many
Of us
So alike
So different
So what.

This I Know For Sure
Sitting too long
In one place
Feeling like the world has passed you by and
Woe is you
Because you're old
Will push
You deeper into the pluff mud
Of nothing
Into more nothing
Until
You
Disappear, but
Doing something
Any something
Will move you
Activate you
And one grows
Into more then
Many and many gets you going again
Nike has it right. You know.
Just do it.

Remember
Long distance calls?
How special they were
How we
Planned them
Looked forward to them
Used them sparingly
Amazing
Miracle of the times.
How I miss those
And hand written
Notes of thanks
Of
Hello How Are You?

Passion
Used to
Drive me
Got me up
To go
To do
Got me up for that too
Knew I could
Energize
When
Needed
Get it done
Make 'em
Applaud
See how good I am. Was.
Where has it gone
Away from me
I can't seem to find it again.
And I had nothing to say about it.

Oldies But Goodies
We listen to
Music that we
Love
Danced
Closely
Whispered
Stuff
That came to be
Doing it
Still
Loving it
Still
Now that we are
Real Oldies
Real Goodies.

Use To Be
just three
and sometimes less
Early morning
Daytime
Till midnight
Cheap entertainment on the tube
Now
Wow!
A Vastland of choices
Twenty four hours
Seven days a week
Three hundred sixty five
Everywhere you look
Listen
So much there.
Not much there.

Afternoon And Early Evening Nods
come
And I can't stop them
Tired run down
Bored, indolent
Snorts wake me
Ashamed when I don't respond
To a question
React to a bogey
Or participate in conversation
It just blindsides me.
Is this the sleep
before the big sleep? Tryouts!!

Little Things
You never thought
To be Hard
Are.
Just getting out of a chair
Without
Soreness
Pain
Grunting
Pushing
Pulling
Regretting
Limitations
That seem to come with the
Territory.
Accepting.

Sides
All
Through
The
Vastland
Countless
Commercials
Telling us
Who to be
How to be
When to be
What to be
And the
Medications
The best of all
Helping
Anew
But

Watch out
For
The sides
Nausea
Headaches
Bloat
Weight loss or gain
Hives
HBP
LBP
Gout
Diarrhea and/or
Constipation
Depression
Anxiety
Mood swings
Lost wages
Shortness
Tallness
Night blindness
Mother in law blues
Mass Murder tendencies
Restlessness
Irritability
Terrorist tendencies
Even Death
And they just go on
And on
Unbelievable!
Not me
Sticking with
What I've got.

Along The Way
Many starts
Many stops
Checking in to see
What was there for me
Found and lost
Lost and found
People
Places
Things
Feelings
Ideas
Beliefs
Hopes
Dreams
Realities

Starts and stops along the way.

Remember that space for you at the back.
Write something there.

3.

Sit Down And Stay A While

                              Visits
                            One, two
                           Three, four
                            Five, six
                         They're monthly
                              now
                          Agreed places
                          Where we go
                            Together
                          Hand In Hand
                         But not in step
                      We never were in step,
                       Thank god for that.
                    But we were definitely in love.

This Is Not Good
You have captured my body. Yet
You have freed it to feel fine tuned, honed
For you and you alone, always ready for
Your touch. Hungry, still after for even more.

     This is not good.

Not only have you captured my body
You have captured my time.
It's all yours. I try to give it somewhere else.
I even do it.
But it's not without you standing close, smiling.

     This is not good.

Not only have you captured my time
You have captured my mind.
It knows the countless things it must attend.
There and energized yes. But never as a single.
You always sing duet.

I even try to push you out, but when the touch,
A grasp instead.

   This is not good.

You have not only captured my body, my time, my mind
You have also captured my soul.
Your light is warm and peaceful. Your glow
Turns my gray and used and tired to renewed hope
Overflowing joy. Belief in so much more.
Colors now and useful once again.

   This is not good.

This is a miracle.

Love Has Not Been a Stranger To Me
I have known her.
She embraced my mother and me
And my father in an entirely different way.

She showed me her way with my brothers and cousins
And aunts and grandmother and friends
although looking back that may have been something else.

As I grew, she showed me more and let me love
A wife in a way that I could then. There was care
And caring but there was always in the way me.

Later, she introduced me to passion and that was good.
And then came romance and then came otherness.

Out of nowhere love matched me to another who knew her in
a different way but a way that made me feel really Loved.
I finally arrived at the ultimate, I thought.
She gave two a connection and a bond and that, too,
was good.

And then she changed course. Love redefined herself.
She became something else. Romance waned. Passion
cooled. Only care remained. And otherness. Confused and
despondent. How could it have become something else?

And now I know. She changed to become that
something else.
Love has gently warmed her way deep into a place I didn't
know existed. She has revealed a part of her that goes way
beyond anything imagined.

She has let me have this time with her
very own incarnation.
She has given me her self.
She has given me you.

Will You Remind Me
to tell them to fix the overhead light in the car?
Who's going to remind me?
Let's leave notes.
Remember to do that.
You remember to do that.
Ok. Ok.

I forgot.
You remembered.
You forgot.
I remembered.

We two do make a good one.

Spooning
The greatest pleasures
And comforts of the day
Any day
Are those when the last light is out
The dogs are quiet
The nite lights are soft
And I snuggle up
And hold you gently firm
Being just where I want to be
then
It's your turn to hold me
Even better.
What a fit!

Bubble Stuff

She called him her "bubble stuff."
He had mixed emotions about it
When they were alone he blushed a bit
smiled and he wanted to rub up against her
cat like, to get whatever else she had.
When she used it in mixed company
even with close family
he would give her a look that said
 "that's private" flush red and retreat to another
room of conversation
or busy himself in the kitchen.
His daughter thought it was cute, and sweet.
She liked that he finally had found someone
that even she adored.

When You Can Stare
at your wife in bed beside you
mouth open, snoring a bit
and you can smile with warmth in your heart
and say to yourself
she's so cute when she does that.
When you can gently smooch the wrinkles
under her chin, brush her crows feet and
mouth lines with your lips and
flash a genuine smile with a
of course I love you, you do.

Finding joy
Was a daily discovery in youth
Except for the disappointments
that came, the hurts, the heartbreaks.
Made me strong and wise
So today I can still have joy
Along with the disappointments,
the hurts, the heartbreaks.

Temptations
Galore.
Sitting there
Staring
Just asking us to take
Eat, drink, buy, speak, risk, try, go, stay, feel, give, keep.
Ignore,
Sure.
Easy,
Not,
Use wisdom,
Ha.
Use will.
Ha. Ha. Ha.

Closer
please
I can't get any closer
Try
She did
And did.

Difficult Getting through The Days
Feeling like no purpose
Tired of doing stuff
I don't really want to do
Tired of going
Just to be going
Tired
Just tired.
Then you come
I smile and want you
Filled with energy
Forgetting tired
That stuff comes from another place.

PDA
Public display of affection
And PDA, Private display of affection.
Either is fine with me
For some, emotion varies
Shy Shame Proud Private Cute Sweet
Well a little hand-holding never hurt anybody.
PDA, Private?
Well now
That's another matter.
Ours

Grandchildren
Come and go
Like our children
Arriving then
Leaving us
behind.
Their life
Their choice
Like we did.

    But before taking off
    What pride
    What angst
    What pain
    What worry
    What joy
    What hopes
    What memories.

Son Told Us Today
That he and family would
Not join us for this holiday
They see us all the time
So they are going
Somewhere else to see
Someone else
They don't see so often
We understand
Completely?
Hello New Rationed Parents

You'll Tell Me
If I have food in my beard
If you'll tell me I have spinach
on my tooth
If I talk too loud
If I talk too much
If I repeat myself
If my jokes aren't funny
If the blackheads show
If the hairs need tweezers
If I eat too fast
If I'm unkind
If I'm fading fast
If I'm still pretty
If I'm still a hunk
Oh, yes. Still.
OK then.
We're fine

We Did Some Things
A place where smiles come easy
The couch a teddy bear for many.

Finding comfort even in discord
Safe enough for honest words.

The time together renews the bond
The people there embrace the you.

There was a hole now pushed way back
Filled in with growth that only time can give.

Gifts and food and care abound
That place we nurture and find again.

They still long to touch the roots
We made it strong, it holds us well.

  Home.

4.

Whose Life Was It Anyway!!

You
You
Are
The
You
In
*You*rself.
Who
Else
Could
Be there?
You
Are
The
One
To think
To say
To do
To be.
Who
Else
Knows you
As you
Know
You?
Only
You.

He Often Envied
those who knew why they had been born.
The natural athlete, or explorers or teachers who never even thought about being anything else. They came to do a certain job, and they did it, got very good at it and were honored for having given their all to the task, or to others.
He could have gone in so many different directions.
He had some talent in many areas...and choosing one or even two proved to be melancholy now in his last years.

He often wondered if he had gone in another direction, what would his life have been like? If he had chosen to pursue his first love, or even his second, would it have made any difference in how he felt now?

Thoughts About It All
Maybe tell her
now that he has been dead for a year
Cancer got him young
Thought about it all
and how dying early
takes care of any
old age second guessing
And wondering
about what comes next
And whether we did
all we wanted to or
we bog down in
Misery of Lost Life
and regrets.
No
Don't
Tell
Her
She knows.

Irritations On The Small Stuff
Come more often and quicker
Impatience with an open drawer
Those ads inserted in magazines
That have to be ripped out
Stickers on my apples
And remains of stickers on my gifts
How thin can they make paper, anyway?
Wasting time trying to turn a page
The dirty dish in the sink
Stacks of stuff in the way
The way she says no now
The way she never says yes
The way he rolls his eyes
The way we turn our backs in bed
In life.

OC
Obsessive Compulsive at 75.
Really!
Just another detail that
Pisses me off
The cleaning lady didn't
Put it back like it was.
A cleaning lady?
This is where
That belongs
Somebody hung my robe on the wrong peg
The towel is not in
The right place
And there's
A place for everything
And everything
In its place
Like me.

Hanger Hell
Just came back from there
Had to clean that closet out
Peel apart those shirts so smashed
Found traffic jams of hangers
Wires entwined with wires
Hooked inside the others
Pull one way, it's so wrong
Pull the other, it's wrong too
Patience needed but there's none left
Feeling blood fill up the face
Maybe pop the pump too soon
Best to take a break for now
Return when time is not a race
Start the cycle once again
Put off the task that's not that great
Those damn things can surely wait

Two Seniors
Giving each other
The middle finger
In the parking lot
At the post office
Both right.
Both wrong.
Does it really matter?
Seems to
To them.

Feel Like Screaming
Unfair
Unjust
Rude
Ignorant
Incompetent
Intolerant
Inconsiderate
Mean
Hands tied
Mouth shut
Inside heat
With no where to go.

          Even
          The
          Most
          Intimate
          Friends
          Never
          Know
          About
          The
          Sagging
          Balls
          In
          The
          Toilet bowl
          Water.

And Then
First with the prostate
Sitting to pee
They don't understand
Standing
Took too long to finish.
Multi stops on trips
Movies not over two hours
Biopsies
Benign
Lucky
But roto rooter
Still sitting
Now challenged by
All low commodes with
High water

This is the age
Where men make
close friends of
urinals

Sagging
Comes
Slowly
But it comes
What was here
Moved to there
Changing waists
Other parts too, not seen
But felt
Hell NO to T- shirts
All tight fitting anythings
Avoiding mirrors
Reflective windows
Anything that shows us to ourselves

Getting Shorter
was
A surprise.
Another
Unexpected
Gift
Of
Aging.

Pretty Soon
I'll get to that
I'll get to that
I'll get to that
And that
And I'll get to that
And that
I'll get to that
I'll get to that
Too
I'll get to that
And I'll get to that
And that
Pretty
Soon
Now.

When You Get Old
Your body starts making noise
Starts talking to you
Snap crackle and pop joints
With vocal accompaniment
Groans, moans, ows and ohs and a few dammits.
Hurts to move
To roll over
To readjust.
It hurts to change positions
and opinions

TV Is My Challenge
So much wrong and
I catch them at it
Yelling at the stupidity
Of officials
Of commercials
Politicians
City officials
Politicians
City officials
Celebrities
Did I say Politicians!
You think that's good!
I think it stinks!
No one cares.
I do.

It Takes Longer
to tie the shoes
Looking, not finding new ways
Bending won't work,
Lifting either,
Sitting on the floor
In a chair on a stool
Crooking the leg
Finally asking for help
Pissed about it, then
Velcro
Slippers
Barefoot!

Expand-a-Waist
pants.
Genius.
Fit like a glove
Pride lost to bulge
Why not expand-a-shirts?
Now go to Goodwill after 20 years.
Button strain shows the gap.
Now, larger size on the cheap.
Breath holding time reduced 20%.

Senior Ballet
One legged
Dancing
Not holding on
Putting foot
In pants
Under wear
Panty hose
Finding balance
Being graceful
And fearful
That it will
Only get worse.

Reinventing Ourselves
is what we're
Supposed to do
But
I like me as I am.

They Laugh At Us
I know. I used to.
We wear strange clothes
They're old
Why get new
They think we have bad taste.
They don't know that we just
Don't give a shit.
We don't deserve it all
Not all.
But some for sure
Loud
Self centered
Selfish
Demanding
Don't listen
Talk
A lot
About
Our lives
Where we came from
What we did
Who we were
When we were.

The Older I Get
the more pissed off I get.
It's no wonder old people get cranky with age
    they see the end
    they didn't get it all done
    they didn't do anything they wanted to do
        much less everything they wanted to do
No time to start over.
Trying to contribute
Get
disrespect
demeaned
discouraged
Pissed off
Like never before.
Saw this poster recently of
a lovely lady and her quote
 "the older I get
the more people can
kiss my ass!"

Bothers Me
People who park
in no parking
handicapped
wrong lane
wrong way
take up two
parking spaces
biggest suv
on the block.
People in movies
putting their feet,
sometimes bare feet! on
the back of the chairs in
front of them,
talking loud
at wrong times
leave during
credits blocking view of
others.
Rudeness
Inconsiderate.
Hard to tolerate rudeness
It's all about that
For me
Pissed off.

Educate Me?
I don't want to know
All that stuff
That will make me
Happier
Healthier
Richer
Wiser
Skinnier
Smarter
Social
I just want to be
Me.

Hair
growing where
It shouldn't
Not growing where
It should.
You know
Hair today
Gone tomorrow.

        Skin Gets Thin
        Letting through those
        Dark places
        The red, black, blue
        Road maps
        That were hiding there
        All along.

All The $ Went
to someone
Not me
And now I sit wishing regretting wondering
mad as hell
sad too
And not knowing
What's next.
Plans I had derailed
Accidents
Fate
Illness
Injury
Things happen
Unintentional detours along the way.
Changes always changes
There's no turning back.
Can rewind and look at it
Pause and reflect on it
But it's done
Can't change what was.
Can change what might be.

Starts With Squinting
while denying
Looking for light
Stretching arms
Holding too close
Giving in
Ends with glasses
Bi, Tri, Thick
Lucky no MD
Thank god for
Big Letters

For A While
I bitch
I moan
I complain
until I see a young man
in a wheelchair
driving it with his chin
and then I realize how lucky I am
       for a while.
I whine
I lament
I yell unfair
until I see a man with cerebral palsy painfully
inching his way down the sidewalk
greeting people with an awkward smile
and then I realize how lucky I am
       for a while.

I get depressed
I become desperate
I panic
until I see a homeless woman shivering
among her full cart of worldly possessions in a dark alley
and then I realize how lucky I am
       for a while.
I see frail
I see fear
I see no hope
In the hollow eyes of old people filed away.

What does it take to be
permanently grateful?
Being a homeless, wheel-chair
moving victim of cerebral palsy?
And becoming frail, fearful, alone and hopeless?
       I hope not.

Reading
TV
Hers
His
Sometimes
His
Hers
Mostly
Each other's
Home life.
It works.

Tired Of Doing It
No, not *that*
We still do that
Some don't believe it.
Tired of pinching pennies
Writing monthly checks
Waiting for a real person on the phone
Waiting for the kids to call
A thank you note ...
From anybody!
Brushing teeth
Combing my hair
Taking pills
Doctor's appointments
Procedures
Required social time
Bridge
Walking at the mall
Shopping
Golf
Drinking
Not remembering
All the good things

Clothes
Comfort not style
Except to
Impress the others at the
Dragged-to
Socials
Meetings
Worships
Weddings
Funerals
A lot.
So few
Look.
Fewer
Care.

Can't Talk About
Hemorrhoids
Gout
Gas
Pimples
Flatulence
Psoriasis
Operations
Procedures
Children
Politics
Religion
Savings
Stock market
Neighbors
In laws
But
We do.

Regimen
Struggle up
often smiling to be
Pee
Robe
Hands, face, hair
Hand cream
Age defying! (Love that one.)
Glasses
Where are they?
Slippers
Kitchen
Coffee
Water
Newspaper outside
TV
Banana
Health bar
Peanut butter on something
Pills, wake up,
not too many,
gurd, or gerd, which?
heart, strength,
vitality, bones, aches,
multi-vision
whatever's left
Coffee
TV
Bathroom

Then
Newspaper
TV

Coffee
Walk
Aquacize Flirt Shower
Office
Calendar
Nothing
Computer
Nothing
Email
Nothing
TV
Nothing
Cereal lunch
Sunday Times
Magazines
Meetings maybe
Walk the dogs
Organize
Reminisce
TV
Plan tomorrow. Tough.
Drinks dinner
TV or rare book
Pre bed
Similar
Post bed
Late TV
Some sleep
Start again
Struggle up
Ahhh
The Good life.

Mom Chose Family Dollar Sweats
Gave her Belk's blouses
that stayed in the boxes
Still the sweats
Why, Mom?
Easier
Finding
Choosing
Maintaining
Cold wash
No iron
Three colors
Black, grey, and navy blue
Soft
Comfy.
We were frustrated
Bewildered
Now we know
how smart she was
Now it's us
Just nicer sweats
More Colors

Growing Apart
It's called now
Growing together
It should be
Could be.

What Have We Become
Where is what we were?
Along the way
The disconnect that
We vowed would not be us
And here we are
Together but
Apart
Wondering
Grieving what was
Hoping
For something else
Something
That was

Again

There Is
No
Bottom
To the
Depth of pain
We feel
When
There is loss
Moms
Dads
Brothers
Sisters
Friends
But the worst
By far
The deepest
Pain
Loss of
Your

Child.

YOUR TURN anytime. Take a break and write about your own memories. Blank pages waiting for you at the back.

5.

Ok. Now What

Beliefs
Practicing what
We preach
Or not.
So many ways
From so many places
BaskinRobbins flavors
It works most of the time
Some think everybody else
Is wrong
Others think the same thing
Similar goals
Heaven not hell
Will we get where?
Up to each.

Home Work
in youth
Chores, self, clothes, room, bed, trash
School
Home work
More school
Home work
Job
Home work
Life
Home work
Living, teaching, growing, failing, falling, moving on
Our own Home
More Work
Our own lives, home work
Still.

Time
it's been going on for some time now
and I think I have learned some things

Here's one

I don't waste as much time as I used to
The process of getting to depression
and coming out again is shorter

I can go to the suicide mode
and up to euphoria almost immediately
without messing around
with all that stuff in between.

Brick By Brick
I build my Wall
Ten feet wide
And
Twice as tall
Yes, I wonder
When they say
That Wall
Is it protecting you
Or
Is it in your way?

Self Help
Book shelves lined with volumes
soul searching philosophy
simple and deeper poetry
for sale psychology
from infomercials.

A lot has helped a little
a little has helped a lot
a storehouse of searching
a library of life

Along with others
I've needed all the help
I could get
to face the unexpected events of life.

    In it all I made a find.

The best single aid for
grief, loss, depression,
frustration, confusion,
rejection, desperation,
anger, hurt, loneliness
and all of the more
is to have a
little money in the bank.

Anthropology Navigator
is what they called it on TV
Not sure if it's real but it makes sense to me
Pilots, sailors, and hard headed
husbands use it too.
Dead Reckoning
explained by them as
to know where you are, you
have to know where you've been,
what it looked like,
felt like,
sounded like,
who you were when
who you wanted to be
Then, you know if you've arrived

The Cloudy Day Parts

It's winter in my heart and I'm gonna spill my guts.
I ask myself, why tell anyone about the shit?
It lets them know I'm human. Too human maybe.
It lets me know I'm not alone. It helps me get rid of it.
It's part of my selfishness.

My mind tells me it's a place I'm in, that's all. It will go away tomorrow. It's happened before. This time, I'm not sure. It feels like it might stay for a while.
Until I make it go away.
This time, I'm scared.

In my early years, I was hugged a lot. Mother, aunts, cousins. It made me feel special and loved. Except my dad. I knew he loved me, he never told me he did. But he acted like it. It gave me some sense of self-worth. I thought.
I had enough in storage to last a long time. Until yesterday.

Now it comes to this. Realities block out the plans I had! It all seemed right. I thought I had a purpose. I was actually going to do something wonderful and memorable.

And now? I've left a trail of sadness, frustration, heartbreak, and regret behind my egocentric self. I thought I was helping. I thought I was giving. I thought I was planting seeds for growth. I thought wrong.

I wasn't smart enough to make it.
My children are confused.
They look to me and I have no truths to tell them.
 I cannot give them guidance.
I am lost myself.

Things came. The winds blew and I went with them.
I've never been able to start the breeze and
follow it through the trees.

The first faint colors of my own mortality have begun to glow around the outer defenses of my living.
Barely visible now, I know they are there.
Breathing down my neck.
Mostly they are shades of foreboding grey. Not those fifty shades, either...did you see that movie? Now that's change! My grey is just one color...dark...
but I have to say...sometimes
and getting more often,
they are pastel and pleasing and inviting.
And they will get brighter and closer.

I don't plan well. So many times I've built a road and on it traveled for a while.
Each time, there were pot holes, mud puddles, and side exits that took me off into a thicket of nothing.
Returning, I would proclaim in pain that the journey was much too rough or something or somebody kept me from my goals. I was good at blaming.

And then I'd build a new road.
And start out again.
Looking.

I have seen talent. I have seen vision. I have seen brilliance. I have seen genius. I have seen greatness.
But of these, I am none.
What, then, am I?

Limbo. It's not a good place.
Waiting for something to happen.
For someone to decide about things that will affect my life. I could just say to hell with them.
But I can't do that. There's too much at stake.
So. I wait. How much longer?

Approval. Accomplishment. Affirmation.
It's been so very long since I've had any.
I used to get it, have it all the time. Then it went away.
I must be doing something wrong.
No one says I like you. My atta boys have disappeared.
On the job. In the home. In the bed.
Not even two shades of grey there.

Rejection scares me most of all. It used to never even enter my mind. I went so long without it and now it hounds me.
No one's applauded me in such a long time.
How am I supposed to live without it?

There is this strong feeling that I need someone in my life. I don't like it. There is no one in my life.
I don't like it.
I'm not stupid. I know l have choices.
We all do, don't we?
How to choose from the choices! Do I choose for me?
It seems that that's what I've done. But I didn't think so.
And that didn't work.

Be more selfish? Or less?
I don't know.

Connected. Connected to the past. To people. To places.
To ways of doing things. There is a sense of honor. Of duty.
Holding on to what I know I knew.
Dare I break the cord that keeps me there?
Dare I take the risk?
Dare I not?

Cloudy days are cold.
The light is covered and I can't see.
But, I know it's there.
I have to punch holes, or light a fire. Or
simply turn on a switch.
I have to do something.
I can only feel good about myself if I am doing something to
feel good about. You've heard that, I'm sure.
I understand that now. I am the only one who cares about
me. Only I can change that.
The first thing I'm going to do is change the way
I say I all the time. Everything is not about me.
Maybe replace it with *you...or others...or them...?*
Can I do that?

Have I used up the source? It was given to me and it's
Kept me ...sane. Not focused. But sane.
I have to tap into the place it was and dig even deeper.
I can't be gone, because I am still here.
I am alive. I am well. I am me and I do want me to be.
To begin again. Climb out of the bowels of depression.
I see sun rays seeping through my closed blinds.
It's out there waiting to make me warm once more.
I just have to go out there and get in it.
I want to say, I'm changed, I'm still me...
and I want to be for you and with you. I'll make more
mistakes, and I'll develop more regrets but
I am not going to die today!

Good Morning!
I love the way a new day feels.
Those few moments when
Yesterday's memories
Are slept into a docile file for later.
When rest gives birth to new eyes
That see a life with energy and hope
And a chance to try again.

When I Started Getting Less Busy
I became less focused and driven.
I didn't know how to handle non hectic
to-do time, and I would forget stuff,
'cause I wasn't pressured to remember.
I would put off stuff, what's the big deal…
like the one I hate most, paying by due
dates. Then getting
angry when they charge
the late fee.
I still do it.
All the time.
I'm in charge here

Staying So long
keeps so much
stuck in
place.
pictures
on walls
nick and nacks
on tables
Shelves crowding
Closets full
of never worn
favorites
No room for more
Stuff accumulates
over time
Even the floors
the doors
Show wear
But
A
Slight
Movement
Brings
Discomfort.
Dogs bark.
Even the
Dust feels
At
Home.

Sitting In A Room
crowded with
interested guests
hanging on to the speaker's
words of wisdom
Except
Me.
Hard to hear
from where I am
6th row.
Ashamed to
cup my hand
to my ear
Both
sure signs
of age
And
Vanity.

Who
Inspires us.
We do!

Not Too Concerned
about our appearance.
Some of us, that is.
We wear old clothes, not spending that
money we may need for older age
not to burden the children and spouses.
We have nothing to gain by looking great
no wo/man's hand to win,
no job to compete for,
no seeking approval from others
since they don't see us anyway
and the young folks say
look at that old fart/ess
with stripes and checks and pants too short and
tights not right and the no style dress and hair a
mess.
And we smile.

Experience Counts For Something
for a while
then it doesn't matter.
Wrong experience
Not new
No E time
Not up to date
Too slow
Too deliberate
Too much trouble.
Still
Experience counts for something
It's ours.

Retiree Envy At The Fall Festival
Night bugs in a stream of light
like snow flakes caught in a whirlwind
just above the handicapped jiffy johnny
drawn by whatever draws them to such

Inside the circus-like tent without stripes other
creatures gathered for the stuff that draws them
to such music mostly from a mixed group of
instruments all not trained to
perfection but good enough

Old and younger, rich and not so much joined
in appreciation of Barber and Copeland and
a short caring conductor with pianist guest
delivered rhapsodies in blue for multi colored
tables decorated for prizes to come

Food and wine and other hidden spirits aplenty
mostly smiles of enjoyment and standing
applause some not fully
present from too much or not enough

And one small boy who could be you,
out of place, stayed quiet and still as in the dark
his focused face was softly lit by something
small beneath the table's edge.

His something.

Flags Of Our Fathers
opened this week.
I went on a rainy afternoon
and it took my breath away.
I didn't cry only because I stopped myself.
And, as almost always,
I was the last to leave the theater.
I even stayed longer than usual as
the lights eased on and the
ushers flowed into the aisles
wielding their brooms and pans
as they pulled the trash barrels
behind them attacking the mess
that was just made mostly by
senior citizens who had just seen
Clint Eastwood's version of another mess
made by roughly the same generation.
Generations often leave messes
for the next ones to clean up.
Is it a law, the order of things or something?
Can we change that?

I'm Not As Good As I Thought I Was
not as smart
not as special.
I don't know what happened.
Hard to admit
we don't know it all
Mother had drawers
too stuffed to open
Why, mom?
Not smart
Doesn't even make sense.
Now
You should see my drawers,
If I could open them.

My Hectic Busy Life
is slowing down now
My plan
As I have the time to think
Often actually clearly
is to think clearly
I am learning that there are many
more people than I
who are more special than I
or who have probably suffered the same
haunting thoughts as I
That they too were special and had
a special contribution to make in their lives
and wonder
if it's too late.

No News
Is good news
Better than
What we see
Hear
Day after
Day after
Day
Printed
Television
Radio
Painting pictures of
How bad it is
How bad it's
going to be
And no
Slowing down
So
No more news for me
I'll make my own
Thank you.

Epiphany On The Roof
Due to age
I had to change the way I do things
no longer strength, athleticism, balance
Now has to be planning,
not taking risks,
taking breaks (endurance noted)
using my brain and staying focused
like not stepping on the electrical cord and
watching my feet slip out from under me and
rolling me off the roof's edge smashing to
the ground in one large grunt with something
broken that will send me to the emergency
room and her into a dither.

While I was creating this new approach to
living longer and taking great pride in my
discovery I lost my focus on the task,
I stepped on the electrical cord.
Nope. I did not slip down. But,
I allowed myself a couple of well phrased
ouch words loud enough for the preacher
outside next door to hear my closing
exclamation of "Jesus Christ!" respond with
"Praise the Lord!"
Then, I heard her coming.
So much for that.

It's Building
The complexity of it all
overwhelms me
paralyzes my brain.
A global community so flat
we can see it all at one time.
Too much to take in.
It freezes me in place.

Finance
Religion
Retail
Public service
Utilities
Law
Manufacturing
That was us then
Who is us now?

Old People Are Problems
We hear that
Of course we are
One of our entitlements?
Should we be?
We can be more the
Solution.
Nobody thinks to ask.
Don't wait.
Tell them
Speak up
Risk it.
What do we have
To lose?

Timing
Reflexes
Waning
Surprising
Reaching for
My wine glass and
Missing
Oops.

Dogs
Einstein and Eleanor Roosevelt.
No kidding.
On the daily walk
As long as the journey was underway
High spirits and jaunty
But when they sensed that we were about to end it and return home
Spirits fell and a meandering delay set in.
As soon as *we* sense the journey
Beginning to end
We slip into depression
Despair
A sense of loss
Rather than enjoying to the fullest
The time on the trip we have left and
One more sniff of what's there.

Inside Work
Outside work
Those parts of us
Connected for
Life
Who knew?
There's
Still time.

Can't Do It
Can't stop
Can't try
Can't go
Get angry
No
Get
Really angry
Mad
Pissed off!
That might help.
Who?

    I Know I'm Right!
    How could this be wrong?
    Why can't everybody Be Like Me?
    Why can't everybody be just like me?
    Mr. Perfect.
    Then we wouldn't have any problems.

    She is smiling.

All My Life
there was this feeling way down deep inside
that I was special.
    All my life
I felt that there was something unique I was
supposed to do.
    All my life
I found myself out of step pretty much
most of the time.
    All my life
I kept looking and listening for the guidance,
the direction, the way.
    All my life
I wondered how it would happen, when it would
happen and how I would handle it.
    All my life
it seemed to be around the next corner.
Hold on a little while longer and you'll find it.
    All my life
the place I thought I was to be wasn't the place
for long enough to be the final place.
    All my life
I actually believed what I was told
that what I ended up choosing would matter.

As we age we find that with rare exceptions
the rank and file common man has little to do
with what happens in the world, but we do
have something to do with what happens in our
hearts.

That's pretty special to me.

Rambling Thoughts

There are days I feel like
I am waking up after a long sleep.
Now that I am slowing down my brain activity and
my physical to-do list, there is more time for me to see
things I haven't noticed in a long time, or never did, or
thought they were too menial to dwell on at the time. I
find myself seeing people, places, and things...behaviors
for the first time.

Things I know.
We all have feelings of wanting recognition,
approval, applause.
Adults and children alike need involvement,
engagement, inclusion, interest, care
and if we don't get it we become
sad, disappointed, resentful, angry, uncooperative, and
we act out in many ways.

Ranting...I've tried that. Done it a lot. It always
seems to end with no results but rather regrets over
embarrassing those around me and myself. I want so
hard to be Atticus Finch. The original. I want to be
emotionally mature, conversationally brilliant, effective
in my convictions and persuasion efforts.

I think I missed that boat.

Our Sweetest Most Loyal Dog
Einstein
in his last days
had courage and desire to stay living
because he loved and was loved so completely.

And Cinnamon had the patience we should all have.
Waiting for hours for just one toss of the ball
so she could gather her energy, embrace her life,
race to win, bring it back, and wait again.
She found that purpose.

I used to laugh under my breath at the way some
old folks dressed. The leisure suits, the matching
nylon sweat suits with the required stripe, or the
twin tee shirts with "I'm with stupid" printed on the
fronts, the Velcro strap shoes, the awful taste in the
matching of clothes, stripes with checks, yellows
with greens, greens with blues (my mother would
croak), those dumb Henry Fonda On Golden Pond
hats, and the list is endless.
I used to think it was because they had no money as
well as no taste. They lived on a fixed income and
couldn't afford nice new clothes and someone to
advise them on what to choose to wear.

Now that I am one of them, it's not money.
We just don't care. Some of us, that is.
We aren't trying to win another's heart, approval,
blessing, promotions, or anything. Why should we
care? Nobody sees us anyway. And if we really
wanted them to, then wearing this stuff is the surest

way to get their attention. What was it they used to tell us as young parents? Children need attention. If they don't get any, they will do something to get it. They would rather have negative attention than no attention at all. Seems to be true for all ages, huh?

This is what happens to us old folks
as we realize that we are going to die.
Not sooner or later, but
sooner than later.
We see it beginning to lift its head yonder
on the horizon and it scares the hell out of
some of us.
We're not ready to go yet.
We still have some fish to fry.
We want to see the grands grow up and
prove that generations do improve
with each cycle.
We want to see if there is something we
can do to change it all and
make it better.
Not only our lives past, but the lives of the
future old people who as
young folks now
have no idea what's ahead of them.
You know what? Neither do I.

Because we have less and less say so, or any power, or any sense of accomplishment or achievement… we do a whole lot of criticizing. Gives us artificial power, a manufactured coping skill to deal with failure or a sense of it at least or makes us feel that we know better. For a while there, as I unconsciously began to feel the pull of time gone and not complete, I started to criticize everything…I mean everything. Well, not her, even though she did do some stuff that drove me crazy, but with her, I bit the bullet. I didn't want to sound like a cantankerous old curmudgeon.

I criticized the hiway construction, a natural target. I didn't think they knew what they were doing. Why did they do this this way instead of that? Just didn't make sense.
The on and off ramps were stupid and the way the SCDOT patched the roads was a joke. And the town crews, forget about it!

I even criticized the new football stadium they were building at our university. It went up impressively but I just knew that they hadn't measured right. The playing field didn't look like it was 100 yards. It couldn't be. I actually laughed at myself for that.
That's when I knew I was getting better…healthier…more hopeful, and that was due to unloading the "to do" plate and finding

center and clarity. I think some people call that aging into wisdom. I hope so. I could use a little wisdom about now.

Last night we watched a video on the life and work and eventual success of Anne Lamott. She was a heavy drinker for years and years and when she finally stopped, she said she saw life completely different. It slowed, it became clear and she not only listened but heard and could focus on what was meaningful and important maybe for the first time.

I feel that way now, but it was the slowing down and rewriting the priority list and wondering what to do with the rest of my few years that changed me. It could have been too much scotch, too, but I don't think so. I never was a drunk...just a regular drinker by habit until my speech slurred a bit and I heard myself and set that wisdom in motion
Putting the glass down and not refilling.

I did do a lot of wrestling with moral, or ethical, or legal decisions. There have been times when I felt I should speak up and say something to someone about what they were or were not doing.
When I lived in Los Angeles, I actually got activated. I used to tell people that they

should not park in a no parking space. Or a handicapped space when they were obviously not. Who were they to do it when others were abiding by the law and being considerate? Most of the time, they told me it was none of my business and to get lost
or just go fuck myself.
I thought it was my business. I still do, but if I took action every time I felt it to be in order, I'd spend the rest of my life swiping at those windmills.

I got out of my car once and started directing like a traffic cop, which I learned when I directed a real one in a Commercial. I un-jammed a parking lot traffic jam. People thought I was nuts but they listened and got un-jammed.

When I lived in New York, I actually chastised a store clerk for being rude and uncooperative. To another customer, not me.

I got an unusual sense of well being, warm satisfaction as I pulled the spurs out of his tiny foot one by one. I was for the first time

in a long time, totally focused on the task. I stopped, bent down, held onto our new dog Eleanor Roosevelt with the leash around the wrist of my left hand and
surgically, I thought, nurtured the pitiful one back to his walking and sniffing.
In those rare times past when I would walk the dogs alone, I would always be in a hurry...I would be walking them on my schedule, at my pace, pulling them and jerking them away from those seemingly endless scents of whatever attracted them and slowed us down. I did to the pups what I did to my children and what I now warn parents about as they try to build some kind of positive
relationship with their mysterious offspring while practicing parenting-on-the-run.

It was my normal state of urgency. I have lived most of my life with a to-do list and I was damned good at getting stuff done. I was raised to believe that you are your work and your achievements are the shining stars of success in our world. I had a work ethic so big I almost choked on it. One of many positives handed down to me by my Dad. Character. That was his big thing. He was the most honest man I ever knew. He worked hard his entire adult life, finally living a few years with his camellias and azaleas before cancer got him at 61. I can't cheat. I can't lie. Well, I can't out and out lie.

Whites and omissions, yeah, but they don't
count in today's world. They counted
to my dad, though.

I gave a workshop once and nobody came.
Not even the person who asked me to do
it. I laughed.
It was all I could do.

Some of My Movie Gems
The Hours.
Someone has to die in order for the rest of us to
value life.
My life has been stolen from me.
I thought it was the beginning of happiness.

You cannot find peace by avoiding life.

Lord of the Rings.
All you have to do now is to decide what to do with
the time
you have been given…

My favorite movie
Atticus Finch (the original one) tells his son
There's a lot of bad stuff in the world.
I can't protect you from it all
Following the guilty sentence of Tom
In To Kill A Mockingbird

I feel guilty just sitting on the couch and

working hard not to have such a full plate. I feel that I have been given some unique talents... at times I even considered myself a renaissance man, but I believe you have to be really outstanding at at least one thing and pretty good at a lot of others to
qualify for that label.
Maybe next time.

People tell me to stop feeling guilty. They tell me to relax and enjoy my last years to the fullest. I have worked and worked hard for over 50 years, which doesn't seem like a lot relatively speaking, but with our life expectancy now about 76 (and 12 of those getting out of high school, another 4 in college, another 3 in the army) you would think that all of those years I worked as
did any red blooded American boy would have been enough. So now I should just quit?
Sure.

Clint Eastwood did some of his best work in his 70s
Now in his 80's and he's still at it!
I'm not gonna just sit around and fade away,
I'll tell you that, right now!

It's interesting what happens to us
as we find ourselves with more time.
Today, I didn't feel stress and
pressures of taking care of the to-do
list items, since there are few left on
the list these days.
So a lot of them fell
Through the cracks. And next month
They will bite me in the ass!

How long do I wait?
At what point do I stop saying
gee whiz, golly, oh my, I'm sorry if I
caused you to misbehave...that you
approach life differently than I...like those
cutting people off in traffic, no signal,
jumping in line.
Insurance companies not paying for
procedures
Medicare mess,

rude and incompetent clerks
politicians who don't get it
no follow up on calls, or activity.
no return calls.
consideration.
polite.
basic manners.
teen age cave men and women.
parents so caught up in their own mess,
have no time, no desire, no clue about
children.

What I want to say is,
WHAT IS WRONG WITH YOU!?
How could you possibly think
that is the way to act!

Wouldn't help.
Would it.

    I have time to stop and talk with neighbors without feeling like I have to hurry and get on to what ever is next.
I had time to go through the dry cereal inventory, sorting out the old

stuff and putting the keepers into attractive plastic containers, and I even tore off the box top so we would know what dwelled therein.

Why do we do that?
Find ways to spend more time on frivolous tasks. Maybe to help us feel a sense of accomplishment, like we really are doing something useful. Something we can actually complete. I know that's why I like to work in the yard, now. I used to hate it,

because I was too busy doing other more important stuff.

You know.

6.

My Time Has Passed

Volunteer
That's what
we do
and we do it well
They need us
They love us
Or not
They want us
To help and
We do
Them.
Us.

Something So Mundane
becoming so important.
Today, I polished my shoes
My black ones, then my brown ones
Buffed my suede ones
New strings in my New Balance all-purpose.
Took my time and did a good job
Didn't feel rushed to get on to something else
Polishing my shoes was the something else
It had been such a long time since
I had done them myself.
Had them done by the shoe shop.
Stuff done by others.
You know, we busy people living
life in the fast lane
like we're supposed to, quick,
always in a hurry,
just touching the surface of
important things,
too often forgetting what mattered, forgetting value.
Like how important it was to have
an unhurried conversation with my son.
Nice shoes?
Lost son.

I Cry Over What Should Be
I cry over what could be.
I cry over what is.
I also cry over what is.
I sometimes laugh.

I'm Not Dead
I'm only resting
Waiting
To see which way I go next
New work
New friends
New place
New peace
Retired.
No
Just resting.

Still Doing
the things I like
going where I can.
Now
There is more
More time
To do and go and be
More of others
More of me.

Who Served?
A pride cry
For those
Who did
The big one
And several after
Some called to
Some wanted to
Most came home different
Too many
Did not
Come home
At all.
Will we always
War?
Will we always
Have to?
Glory in winning
With sacrificial loss
Makes
Way for the
Next one.

We Matter
Just when I thought I knew it all
I didn't
Just when I thought I was tall
I came up short
Just when I was on top
I fell
Just when I was loved
I lost
Just when I gave up
I got up
We matter.

So
Here I am An old person. Are you yet? Now in the elder ranks...a position in life. I, for one, accept.
Because now, when someone asks me to do something, I say. Sorry, Elders don't do. We advise, we consult, we point things out... things like, she doesn't look 60 to me...more like 80! Or,
don't go anywhere with him, he drives like a mad man, And he'll hit on you, if you give him a chance, or even some more serious observations, like

- A. That place in darkness when the lights come on
- B. He lost his strengths trying to improve his weaknesses
- C. That thud on the roof, it's a limb from a tree. Got tired of hanging on, so it just let go.
- D. We point to leaves falling gently from trees, floating, taking their time, a choice to let go with dignity.

As elders in our gained wisdom, we have all the answers, you know. We feel obligated to share those answers with you, some of them at least. Ones that always worked best like

Huh? You asking me? Beats me dude. I haven't a clue. What are you talking about? How the hell should I know? Damn good question. It's a mystery to me. As De Niro would say...You talkin to me? Whoever knows, really? Run that by me again.
And the best of all
Go ask your mother...your grandmother!

Elder wisdom ain't what it's cracked up to be.

They've Gone Under.
A good phrase for it
For the awfulness
Of a small business owner
Losing her/his
Investment
Savings
Relationships
Credit
Pride
Security
Dream.
So many in our lifetime
Gone under.
Pure sadness.
I went under
Once
Was enough.

There's A Picture Of Me
holding my 18 month-old son in my arms
at the beach on vacation
both in our bathing suits.
I was comforting this sandy child
who was obviously in some sort of
toddler distress.
The picture is one of many on my screen
saver and every time I see it
I dwell on it for as long as I can
thinking wondering
how different things would be now if
I could only go back to that time
and start again.

When We Start Reflecting
on our lives
what we did what we didn't do
what regrets we have
what we would have done differently
had we had the chance
we can either nose dive into depression and
wallow there until we slowly deteriorate
or we can see the past for what it is
when we made choices, decisions
took roads we thought were best
making them on the knowledge
the information we had at the time.
Turns out some of that knowledge
was incomplete
made complete only
in the living of life
over a life time
and the information was tainted
by others who were also
traveling on roads that
were decided incorrectly for them.
Either way we have
to deal with the oncoming end.
Some of us want to live it out
no matter what the quality
since we are always teachers and learners
even in death.
There are reasons for being
here until we're not.
Others of us want only to end
the pain the despair that we feel
that we most likely
will cause our loved ones
left to take care of us and
our disarrayed lives.
That's when we think about
how we will cleverly end
it all.

Spending 10 or 20 percent of our days
thinking about how we could off ourselves
so nobody will know so the insurance will be paid
seems to be a total waste of the time we have.

We Are Here To Grow
together,
to mutate,
to meld,
to mesh into one human race
one in love,
in care,
in belief,
in thought,
in word,
in deed and
in spirit.
Then we will be one with the creator…
the universal energy that
has split us all apart like a big bang
to see if and when we will ever
find our way back
to wholeness.

Or we could be meant to be
A diverse hodge podge of humanity
Trying to figure it out dealing with all the
Crap it brings just being here.

 Who knows?

Waiting
For what?
Lose weight
Feel better
Better time
Miss my show
Too much
Wrong day
Trouble
Tired
Angry
Sad
Depressed
Too late.
Do it now
Don't wait
Could be
Too
Late.

    When You Have Nothing To do
      And
      It
      Doesn't
      Bother
      You
      It's
      Hard to find
      Something
      You
      Want
      To do.

Criticize.
Easy to do
Hard to take

So Much To Do
So much to still learn
So much noise of knowledge
And pressures to catch up
From outside
Inside
Knowledge
Gone
Wild
Overwhelm and
Exhaustion.
Love my naps.

Gone.
Work, routine, structure, salt, red meat, chips,
ice cream, pimento cheese, hamburgers,
calories, coffee,
alcohol, snacks, cigarettes, etc. etc.
What's left?
Life.
Lost what?
Found what?
What do you think?
Where were you?
Where are you now?

Paralyzed
in memories
Stuck in the past
Nothing but fear
of what's not there
Of what's not known.
What am I going to do today?
Nothing.
I've already done that.

Took The Less Traveled Path
No one knew what they were doing
Although brave.
Took the most traveled path
Not many knew there either.
Keep guessing.
Keep trying.
There might be an answer.

Will
To avoid
The stuff that could cut my life shorter
Will to do what I know to do
Can't find it
Where's will.
I've lost will.
What else you got?

Three Things
to take with me
Laid side by side to remember
Later there
Remembered only two.
Need
A better plan.

Here's One
Senior senior
Walking down
The sidewalk
Head down
Into phone
Texting!
Given a wide path
Helping hands to
Oblivious
High on Hi tech
Senior futurist
Working out.

Anger
Deal with it
Can't stuff
It will go
Somewhere else
Inside
Outside
All around
Can't stay
Has to go
Has to be.
How
Where
When
Are
The
Hard parts.

What I Owe
What to give back
OK. What?
Nothing
Got nothing
Gave nothing
Dissatisfied
Depressed
Slow death
In place
What's left?
Alternatives
Self a mess
Wake up call
Opportunities
Not problems
Find value
Find purpose
Now's the time.
What we've
Already done
Doesn't really matter.
What we have left to do
Does.
There are
Things
We
Can
Do
That
We
Should
Have
Already
Done
And
Can
Do
Now.

Luck

What's luck got to do with it?
Is there any such thing?
Luck be a lady
Lucky break
Lucky me
Lucky you
Luck smiled on her
Lucky they got to where they were going
Before…
Some people got it
Some people don't
Do you think it's so?
Answer this
Does
Luck
Run
Out?

7.

The Road Most Travel

The Only Way
I can make it now day to day is
to believe that
all of it, everything
that happens
the good the bad
are part of the larger picture
the grand design
the ultimate truth
the final secret
the revelation of divine purpose
the coming together of it all as one.
Otherwise I would have given up long ago
when it all started seeming too real
unfair, inconsiderate, without purpose
with no meaning and downright hateful!
The enormous pain and agony suffered
by most of humanity. What could
possibly be the reasons?
The world is taught about the love a heavenly
father has for his children and it has become
more and more difficult to see
how that love and our hate, agony, desperate
mean lives could possibly coexist even
if a divine all-powerful creator makes it so.
I'm feeling it, thinking it is, not knowing it
but it does help me better understand and
accept and believe
something.
But I don't have to like it.
I don't think I'm supposed to.

Best Friends
come
and go.
Only the right ones
stay.
You are one.
My best one.
Stay.

New Best Friends
Pharmacists
Receptionists
Appointment makers
Cashiers
Bag boys
Technicians
Mechanics
Handy men
Docs
Nurses
Walkers
Hired Help
Meds
All of them
Stay.

One
Two
Three
Docs for me
And then
Four more
Enough!
No more.
How
Many
Needed
To say
What we know
Well,
You're just getting old.
What do I owe you, doc?

We Don't Know It
Until we get here
how life is so short.
Now we know to
Be selective
Don't waste time
With the little that
we have left.
Choose carefully
Don't diddle daddle!
oh, and don't forget to ask your
doctor if you're healthy enough
to not diddle daddle!

When Her Mother Was Sick
and on her way out
She was there
Day and night and
In between.
Little things
Big things
Silly things
Serious things
Clean and dirty things
Holding hands
Sharing tears
And memories
Of mostly good
Loving dedication to
Pay back what she got.
She was called
The Angel
When she's ready
Who will her angel be

Maybe me.

Thinking
>Of those
>Who have gone
>before
>Missing some
>Ashamed at
>not missing others
>Parents
>Friends
>Work mates
>Wives
>Husbands
>Brothers
>Sisters
>Aunts and uncles
>Some cousins
>So many.
>Waiting for
>One of them
>To tell me
>What's next.

Old Folks Are Slow To Panic
about dying
We don't worry too much
about that part
It's the
Going.
The how.
The when.
The how long.
The what's been.
The what's left.

Children
making adult decisions
bring adult decisions
for adults to make
for children.
Denying
Blaming
Dividing
Fading
Losing
Regretting
Crying
Dying.

Ailments Abound
with
Cholesterol
Kidney
Heart
Liver
Stomach
Pancreas
Breast
Teeth stuff
No teeth stuff
Cervix
Knees
Hips
And all their meds lined up in a row
How pretty our gardens grow
Ain't life grand!

Friends No More
It's difficult to even see him now
Where did he go
That guy I knew
Disappeared
Into his anger
His regrets
His losses
His sadness
And I can't seem
To bring him
Home.

Getting Harder To Remember
to take all those pills
Got a daily dose box
Didn't help
forgot where I put it.
Wondered
If missing days
Of doses would
Kill me
Nope
I'm still here
And I'm gonna make the most of it
even if it kills me.

Visiting Questions Unanswered
Do you know me?
Do you want me to stay and visit with you?
Do you want to watch the game with me?
Our team remember?
Do you want me to go?
Do you want me to raise your head
so you can see better?
Do you want me to go away?
I won't go far
See you next time.

All The Time We Hear It
        Fixed income
        Tight budget
        Simplify
        Downsize
        Next
        All that's left,
        potato chips and
        A walk in closet.

She Faded
We watched her
not understanding why
she didn't
get up
do something
get out
enjoy life.
We understand
Why
Now.

Giving Up Giving In
Digging in
Staying put
Don't want to
Don't need to
Why should I
Won't matter
Leave me be
But don't forget to love me.
Still.

What You Put In
is what you get out
Heard that Baloney
Put in years
Got back months
If that
Put in time
Got back less
Put in dollars
Got back pennies
Put in love
Got back loss
What you put in
Is what you put in.
What you get back is
up to you.

Place
It keeps changing
There's the
Back Place
The
Future Place
The
Same Place
The
Hoped for Place
And there's
The
Now Place.
The Place
We are is
Now.

How We Do It
depends
On where we came from
Who was there
What it was like
What they did
What they didn't do
What we did
What we have
    Somebody
    Dollars
    Support
    Community
Who we have become and mostly
How we feel about who we have become."

She Settled In To Die
No action
No friends
No work, no play
Endless TV
Too little sleep.
Easy for us to say
Get out
Do this
Do that
Try
She didn't
She just didn't.
Guess what?

Home
It's where the start is
Place of love and care
For growing and knowing
Finding
Becoming
Leaving
Visiting
Less and less
Making
Another home
Filling it
Learning
Growing
Searching
Leaving
Looking for heart
Found some
Lost some
Lost heart
Lost self
Back
At the
Start
Looking for
Home.
It's where the heart is.
Heart.
It's where the home is.

Everybody will be telling us
what to do!
Our children will want to be
our parents
giving orders
commands!
Don't Take It
Let 'em have it!
Don't let 'em have it!
Stand your ground
There's a lot to lose
Freedom
Pride
Checkbook
Keys
Home
Self
Life.
Hold on to what you got
Till you don't.

Dependents
Used to be
My children
At tax time
Now
It's us
On them
At their time
Just doesn't seem right
to me."

Love Life
Sure
It's the only one we've got
Sure?
This time
Not sure
Maybe more.

Last Night
Like many other nights
Of late
In deep dark
Sleeplessness
Replays of
Days and
Years
Toss and tumble me
Inside
With frowns mostly
Some smiles
Regrets and
Successes
A few
Mostly gone.
And now
Up ahead
Seeing those who
Are there already
There.
Almost gone
In those places where
They don't want to be.
What's going on?
The lives
They live now.
Their eyes tell so much
Make me wonder
Can I do that?
Be there.
Go there?

I'm Not Ready
Going to school again
Almost every day
Learning how things got this way
Polite was how we were
At least most times to
Strangers, sometimes family, too.
"Please Wait" was an apology for
The line too long, the clerk engaged,
The plea from a soldier going to war
leaving his sweetheart behind
please wait for me,
Please wait till I can answer,
Please wait a moment,
Please wait your turn,
Please wait and see, use patience please.
Now, TVs, computers, smart phones, tech help on
line Electronic things are always telling us
"Please Wait."
For what? Who knows why?
They've grown so large we
Can't get in when it's best for us to try.
We pay the price to have it now but it
Comes when they are ready.
Please Wait they say with Please to
Make it nice, they think. Frustration
Annoyance, impatience, confusion is what
they get.
I'm using it for training now for
when time comes to claim me,
Your turn now, so I can say, sorry
I'm not ready.

Please Wait.

Don't Care For Me (think Argentina)
dearest Tina
I know that I can do it.
I may be old now, but I'm not dead yet,
I still have breath left, don't take it from me.

Don't wait on me dearest Tina
the truth is, I am still able
to set the table,
boil, cut, peel, cook and sew

Don't cry for me dearest Tina
I know you 'aughter,
'cause you're my daughter,
but it's too soon now,
I'm just not ready,
cant' do this to you...

Fear Is A Scary Thing
What's next
Who's next
What corner do we turn to find what's best.
Who to trust?
Doctors
Lawyers
Politicians
Relatives
Brokers
Companies
Hospitals
Don't let them get you down.
We're here still
Alive still
Smart still,
Most of the time.

About That Doctor Thing
We all have a few, a few too many!
Some seem to care more than others.
To pay the bill they run us through, like
Lucy's candies on the factory tread mill...
but to be fair, some take the time to hear
us out, about the pain
the misery that won't stay away.
Some are even helpful with
meds and advice...like
when my breath got shorter and
my legs moved slow, my doctor said,
you need to lighten your load. So
clean out your purse!!

How To Keep Going
To not give up
Find the
Spark
Hope
Strength
Courage
Desire.
We have known
Hard times
Young ones
Don't know
Don't want to hear it
Oh what marvels we could share
Oh what input to avoid
Pot holes
Walls
Ditches
Fires
Losses
Grief
Lots of grief.
How do we do it
Day after day after day?
That's just us.

Clichés
It's never too late
Get a new lease on life
Everything's gonna be alright
You're only as young as you feel
Get up, get going
Don't worry about it
Help is just around the corner
Blue skies are up ahead
It's not the years in your life
but the life in your years
Live every day like it's your last
It ain't over till it's over.
Helpful
Not a bit.
Sometimes it IS over
Before it's over.

That part.

Let's Say
tomorrow is the last day
For everybody
What would you do
Today
What would you want
Today to be
For me
A soft rain
Falling quietly
From slightly
Cooled grey
Skies
Scotch on the
Side table
Light
Classical
Piano on
Time Warner Music
Candles lighting us
Both in
Cozies
Lying
In bed
Waiting
Holding
Remembering
Thankful.

Closets
Attics
Basements
Storage
All that stuff
Gathered.
Go through it
Clean it out
Like the clutter
In life.
Who's interested
Who cares
Not the kids
Why put them through it?
There are some things
That are hard to trash
Ok with replacement
Some new stuff
But don't throw out the old
It is us.

Rock. But don't rock away!

That's It.

Or is It?

YOUR TURN. I hope you will use these pages to remember your own lives past, and plans for tomorrow. If you are one of those who doesn't write in your books, ok, but please find some paper, a composition book, a journal with empty pages inviting your thoughts and creativity you might have yet to discover. Thank you for reading. And for writing.

Jim R. Rogers. That's me. An 80 year old grandfather of four boys and the father of two men and a woman. My marriage to Sally Z. Hare changed my life, gave new meaning and new directions to my search for questions and answers.
You don't have to marry her to find your own.
Just keep looking.

After graduating from UNC Chapel Hill and 3 years in the Army, I worked in television, advertising and as a commercial director in Charlotte, Atlanta, New York City, and in Los Angeles before changing careers and becoming a Parenting and Family Life Educator, working in inner city Los Angeles and then back in the Southeast and Coastal Carolina University.

Now with the company that Sally and I own and operate, still learning, inc., I am still working with parents and families as they try to find the way toward the most effective parenting they can offer their children. I was a columnist for a regional specialty newspaper for 20 years and published a collection of my parenting and family essays from those years,
"The Incredible Importance of Effective Parenting:
Plain Talk About Raising Children From a
Concerned Field Worker"

"Looking Around" is my second book of poetry, very different from Starts and Stops but even more of what you might find yourself writing.

This first offering of very free verse poems and scattered narrative, *Starts And Stops Along The Way,* is in part a personal memoir, observations, opinions and philosophies, hopes and dreams, successes and failures of a life lived so far and in sharing I invite others on the same journey to continue working toward making your lives a joy to live and to remember to stay connected with
your best traveling partner,
yourself.
Thank you for reading and writing with me.

Jim
jimrogers@sc.rr.com

Write here. Now.

How Was That

www.ingramcontent.com/pod-product-compliance
Lightning Source LLC
Chambersburg PA
CBHW020653300426
44112CB00007B/360